THIS BOOK BELONGS TO

NAME

DATE

"YOU ARE FEARFULLY AND WONDERFULLY MADE"
PSALM 139:14

PSALM 9:9-10

The LORD is a refuge for the oppressed, a stronghold in times of trouble. Those who know your name trust in you, for you, LORD, have never forsaken those who seek you.

TODAY IS _____

DEAR GOD,
THANK YOU FOR:

PEOPLE TO PRAY FOR:

SCRIPTURE READING:

SCRIPTURE REFLECTION:

SELF IMPROVEMENT:

LONG TERM GOALS:

SHORT TERM GOALS:

JAMES 5:16

Therefore confess your sins to each other and pray for each other so that you may be healed. The prayer of a righteous person is powerful and effective.

TODAY IS _____

DEAR GOD,

The LORD will
fight for you;
you need only
to be still.

EXODUS 14:14

TODAY IS _____

THANK YOU, LORD FOR:

PEOPLE IN NEED OF PRAYER

ANSWERED PRAYER:

WORKING ON:

SCRIPTURE:

SONGS/HYMNS:

CALLS TO ACTION
(WHO WILL I SERVE/UPLIFT TODAY?)

ANSWER ME WHEN
I CALL TO YOU,
MY RIGHTEOUS GOD.
GIVE ME RELIEF FROM
MY DISTRESS;
HAVE MERCY ON ME
AND HEAR MY
PRAYER.

PSALM 4:1

TODAY IS _____

DEAR GOD,
THANK YOU FOR:

PEOPLE TO PRAY FOR:

SCRIPTURE READING:

SCRIPTURE REFLECTION:

SELF IMPROVEMENT:

LONG TERM GOALS:

SHORT TERM GOALS:

YOU WILL PRAY TO HIM,
AND HE WILL HEAR
YOU,
AND YOU WILL FULFILL
YOUR VOWS.

JOB 22:27

TODAY IS _____

DEAR GOD,

PROVERBS 15:8

The LORD detests the sacrifice of the wicked, but the prayer of the upright pleases him.

TODAY IS _____

THANK YOU, LORD FOR:

PEOPLE IN NEED OF PRAYER

ANSWERED PRAYER:

WORKING ON:

SCRIPTURE:

CALLS TO ACTION
(WHO WILL I SERVE/UPLIFT TODAY?)

SONGS/HYMNS:

THEREFORE,
I WANT THE MEN
EVERYWHERE TO
PRAY, LIFTING UP
HOLY HANDS
WITHOUT ANGER
OR DISPUTING.

I TIMOTHY 2:8

TODAY IS _____

DEAR GOD,
THANK YOU FOR:

PEOPLE TO PRAY FOR:

SCRIPTURE READING:

SCRIPTURE REFLECTION:

SELF IMPROVEMENT:

LONG TERM GOALS:

SHORT TERM GOALS:

Who shall separate us
from the love of Christ?
Shall trouble or hardship
or persecution or famine or
nakedness or danger
or sword?

ROMANS 8:35

TODAY IS _____

DEAR GOD,

MAY MY PRAYER BE
SET BEFORE YOU LIKE
INCENSE;
MAY THE LIFTING UP
OF MY HANDS BE
LIKE THE EVENING
SACRIFICE.

PSALM 141:2

TODAY IS _____

THANK YOU, LORD FOR:

PEOPLE IN NEED OF PRAYER

ANSWERED PRAYER:

WORKING ON:

SCRIPTURE:

CALLS TO ACTION
(WHO WILL I SERVE/UPLIFT TODAY?)

SONGS/HYMNS:

ROMANS 8:26

In the same way, the Spirit helps us in our weakness. We do not know what we ought to pray for, but the Spirit himself intercedes for us through wordless groans.

TODAY IS _____

DEAR GOD,
THANK YOU FOR:

PEOPLE TO PRAY FOR:

SCRIPTURE READING:

SCRIPTURE REFLECTION:

SELF IMPROVEMENT:

LONG TERM GOALS:

SHORT TERM GOALS:

Be strong and courageous.
Do not be afraid or
terrified, for the LORD
your God goes with you;
He will never leave you nor
forsake you.

DEUTERONOMY 31:6

TODAY IS _____

DEAR GOD, _____

Devote yourselves
to prayer,
being watchful and
thankful.

COLOSSIANS 4:2

TODAY IS _____

THANK YOU, LORD FOR:

PEOPLE IN NEED OF PRAYER

ANSWERED PRAYER:

WORKING ON:

SCRIPTURE:

CALLS TO ACTION
(WHO WILL I SERVE/UPLIFT TODAY?)

SONGS/HYMNS:

One of those days
Jesus went out to a
mountainside to pray,
and spent the night
praying to God.

LUKE 6:12

TODAY IS _____

DEAR GOD,
THANK YOU FOR:

PEOPLE TO PRAY FOR:

SCRIPTURE READING:

SCRIPTURE REFLECTION:

SELF IMPROVEMENT:

LONG TERM GOALS:

SHORT TERM GOALS:

FOR THE SPIRIT
GOD GAVE US DOES
NOT MAKE US
TIMID, BUT GIVES
US POWER,
LOVE AND
SELF-DISCIPLINE.

2 TIMOTHY 1:7

TODAY IS _____

DEAR GOD,

1 CHRONICLES 16:11

Look to the LORD and his strength; seek his face always.

TODAY IS _____

THANK YOU, LORD FOR:

PEOPLE IN NEED OF PRAYER

ANSWERED PRAYER:

WORKING ON:

SCRIPTURE:

CALLS TO ACTION
(WHO WILL I SERVE/UPLIFT TODAY?)

SONGS/HYMNS:

"MY GRACE IS SUFFICIENT FOR YOU, FOR MY POWER IS MADE PERFECT IN WEAKNESS." THEREFORE I WILL BOAST ALL THE MORE GLADLY ABOUT MY WEAKNESSES, SO THAT CHRIST'S POWER MAY REST ON ME. THAT IS WHY, FOR CHRIST'S SAKE, I DELIGHT IN WEAKNESSES, IN INSULTS, IN HARDSHIPS, IN PERSECUTIONS, IN DIFFICULTIES. FOR WHEN I AM WEAK, THEN I AM STRONG.

2 CORINTHIANS 12:9-10

TODAY IS _____

DEAR GOD,
THANK YOU FOR:

PEOPLE TO PRAY FOR:

SCRIPTURE READING:

SCRIPTURE REFLECTION:

SELF IMPROVEMENT:

LONG TERM GOALS:

SHORT TERM GOALS:

THEREFORE, MY DEAR BROTHERS AND SISTERS, STAND FIRM. LET NOTHING MOVE YOU. ALWAYS GIVE YOURSELVES FULLY TO THE WORK OF THE LORD, BECAUSE YOU KNOW THAT YOUR LABOR IN THE LORD IS NOT IN VAIN.

1 CORINTHIANS 15:58

TODAY IS _____

DEAR GOD,

PSALM 144:1

Praise the Lord,
my Rock,
who trains me for war,
who trains me for battle.

TODAY IS _____

THANK YOU, LORD FOR:

PEOPLE IN NEED OF PRAYER

ANSWERED PRAYER:

WORKING ON:

SCRIPTURE:

CALLS TO ACTION
(WHO WILL I SERVE/UPLIFT TODAY?)

SONGS/HYMNS:

What then shall we say
to these things?
If God is for us,
who can be against us?

ROMANS 8:31

TODAY IS _____

DEAR GOD,
THANK YOU FOR:

PEOPLE TO PRAY FOR:

SCRIPTURE READING:

SCRIPTURE REFLECTION:

SELF IMPROVEMENT:

LONG TERM GOALS:

SHORT TERM GOALS:

THEN YOU WILL CALL ON ME AND COME AND PRAY TO ME, AND I WILL LISTEN TO YOU.

JEREMIAH 29:12

TODAY IS _____

DEAR GOD,

ROMANS 12:12

*Rejoice in hope,
be patient in tribulation,
be constant in prayer.*

TODAY IS _____

THANK YOU, LORD FOR:

PEOPLE IN NEED OF PRAYER

ANSWERED PRAYER:

WORKING ON:

SCRIPTURE:

CALLS TO ACTION
(WHO WILL I SERVE/UPLIFT TODAY?)

SONGS/HYMNS:

DO NOT BE ANXIOUS
ABOUT ANYTHING,
BUT IN EVERY
SITUATION, BY PRAYER
AND PETITION,
WITH THANKSGIVING,
PRESENT YOUR
REQUESTS TO GOD.

PHILIPPIANS 4:6

TODAY IS _____

DEAR GOD,
THANK YOU FOR:

PEOPLE TO PRAY FOR:

SCRIPTURE READING:

SCRIPTURE REFLECTION:

SELF IMPROVEMENT:

LONG TERM GOALS:

SHORT TERM GOALS:

"CALL TO ME AND
I WILL ANSWER YOU
AND TELL YOU GREAT
AND UNSEARCHABLE
THINGS YOU DO NOT
KNOW."

JEREMIAH 33:3

TODAY IS _____

DEAR GOD,

"AH, SOVEREIGN LORD, YOU HAVE MADE THE HEAVENS AND THE EARTH BY YOUR GREAT POWER AND OUTSTRETCHED ARM. NOTHING IS TOO HARD FOR YOU."

JEREMIAH 29:12

TODAY IS _____

THANK YOU, LORD FOR:

PEOPLE IN NEED OF PRAYER

ANSWERED PRAYER:

WORKING ON:

SCRIPTURE:

SONGS/HYMNS:

CALLS TO ACTION
(WHO WILL I SERVE/UPLIFT TODAY?)

DEUTERONOMY 20:4

For the LORD your God is the one who goes with you to fight for you against your enemies to give you Victory.

TODAY IS _____

DEAR GOD,
THANK YOU FOR:

PEOPLE TO PRAY FOR:

SCRIPTURE READING:

SCRIPTURE REFLECTION:

SELF IMPROVEMENT:

LONG TERM GOALS:

SHORT TERM GOALS:

Truly I tell you,
if you have faith as small as
a mustard seed,
you can say to this mountain,
'Move from here to there,'
and it will move.
Nothing will be impossible
for you.

MATTHEW 17:20

TODAY IS _____

DEAR GOD,

Therefore put on the full armor of God, so that when the day of evil comes, you may be able to stand your ground, and after you have done everything, to stand.

EPHESIANS 6:13

TODAY IS _____

THANK YOU, LORD FOR:

PEOPLE IN NEED OF PRAYER

ANSWERED PRAYER:

WORKING ON:

SCRIPTURE:

CALLS TO ACTION
(WHO WILL I SERVE/UPLIFT TODAY?)

SONGS/HYMNS:

BUT THOSE WHO HOPE
IN THE LORD WILL
RENEW THEIR STRENGTH.
THEY WILL SOAR ON
WINGS LIKE EAGLES;
THEY WILL RUN AND
NOT GROW WEARY,
THEY WILL WALK AND
NOT BE FAINT.

ISAIAH 40:31

TODAY IS _____

DEAR GOD,
THANK YOU FOR:

PEOPLE TO PRAY FOR:

SCRIPTURE READING:

SCRIPTURE REFLECTION:

SELF IMPROVEMENT:

LONG TERM GOALS:

SHORT TERM GOALS:

PSALM 46:1

God is our refuge and strength, an ever-present help in trouble.

TODAY IS

DEAR GOD,

Cast all your anxiety
on Him
because he cares
for you.

1 PETER 5:7

TODAY IS _____

THANK YOU, LORD FOR:

PEOPLE IN NEED OF PRAYER

ANSWERED PRAYER:

WORKING ON:

SCRIPTURE:

CALLS TO ACTION
(WHO WILL I SERVE/UPLIFT TODAY?)

SONGS/HYMNS:

SO I SAY TO YOU:
ASK AND IT WILL BE GIVEN
TO YOU;
SEEK AND YOU WILL FIND;
KNOCK AND THE DOOR WILL BE
OPENED TO YOU.
FOR EVERYONE WHO ASKS
RECEIVES;
THE ONE WHO SEEKS FINDS;
AND TO THE ONE WHO KNOCKS,
THE DOOR WILL BE OPENED.

LUKE 11:9-10

TODAY IS _____

DEAR GOD,
THANK YOU FOR:

PEOPLE TO PRAY FOR:

SCRIPTURE READING:

SCRIPTURE REFLECTION:

SELF IMPROVEMENT:

LONG TERM GOALS:

SHORT TERM GOALS:

Consider it pure joy,
my brothers and sisters,
whenever you face trials of
many kinds, because you
know that the testing of your
faith produces perseverance.
Let perseverance finish its
work so that you may be
mature and complete, not
lacking anything.

JAMES 1:2-4

TODAY IS _____

DEAR GOD,

WHEN YOU PRAY,
GO INTO YOUR ROOM,
CLOSE THE DOOR AND
PRAY TO YOUR FATHER,
WHO IS UNSEEN.
THEN YOUR FATHER,
WHO SEES WHAT IS
DONE IN SECRET,
WILL REWARD YOU.

MATTHEW 6:6

TODAY IS _____

THANK YOU, LORD FOR:

PEOPLE IN NEED OF PRAYER

ANSWERED PRAYER:

WORKING ON:

SCRIPTURE:

CALLS TO ACTION
(WHO WILL I SERVE/UPLIFT TODAY?)

SONGS/HYMNS:

MATTHEW 11:28

*Come to me,
all you who are weary
and burdened,
and I will give you rest.*

TODAY IS _____

DEAR GOD,
THANK YOU FOR:

PEOPLE TO PRAY FOR:

SCRIPTURE READING:

SCRIPTURE REFLECTION:

SELF IMPROVEMENT:

LONG TERM GOALS:

SHORT TERM GOALS:

All Scripture is God-breathed and is useful for teaching, rebuking, correcting and training in righteousness, so that the servant of God may be thoroughly equipped for every good work.

2 TIMOTHY 3:16-17

TODAY IS _____

DEAR GOD,

I WILL INSTRUCT
YOU AND TEACH
YOU IN THE WAY
YOU SHOULD GO; I
WILL COUNSEL YOU
WITH MY LOVING
EYE ON YOU.

PSALM 32:8

TODAY IS _____

THANK YOU, LORD FOR:

PEOPLE IN NEED OF PRAYER

ANSWERED PRAYER:

WORKING ON:

SCRIPTURE:

CALLS TO ACTION
(WHO WILL I SERVE/UPLIFT TODAY?)

SONGS/HYMNS:

1 TIMOTHY 6:12

Fight the good fight of the faith. Take hold of the eternal life to which you were called when you made your good confession in the presence of many witnesses.

TODAY IS _____

DEAR GOD,
THANK YOU FOR:

PEOPLE TO PRAY FOR:

SCRIPTURE READING:

SCRIPTURE REFLECTION:

SELF IMPROVEMENT:

LONG TERM GOALS:

SHORT TERM GOALS:

EVEN THOUGH I WALK
THROUGH THE
DARKEST VALLEY,
I WILL FEAR NO EVIL,
FOR YOU ARE WITH
ME; YOUR ROD AND
YOUR STAFF,
THEY COMFORT ME.

JEREMIAH 29:12

TODAY IS _____

DEAR GOD,

CONTINUE PRAYING,
KEEPING ALERT,
AND ALWAYS
THANKING GOD.

COLOSSIANS 4:2

TODAY IS _____

THANK YOU, LORD FOR:

PEOPLE IN NEED OF PRAYER

ANSWERED PRAYER:

WORKING ON:

SCRIPTURE:

CALLS TO ACTION
(WHO WILL I SERVE/UPLIFT TODAY?)

SONGS/HYMNS:

PROVERBS 3:5-6

Trust in the LORD with all your heart and lean not on your own understanding; in all your ways submit to him, and he will make your paths straight.

TODAY IS _____

**DEAR GOD,
THANK YOU FOR:**

PEOPLE TO PRAY FOR:

SCRIPTURE READING:

SCRIPTURE REFLECTION:

SELF IMPROVEMENT:

LONG TERM GOALS:

SHORT TERM GOALS:

The Lord will march out
like a strong soldier;
he will be excited like a
man ready to fight a war.
He will shout out the
battle cry and defeat
his enemies.

ISAIAH 42:13

TODAY IS _____

DEAR GOD,

2 CORINTHIANS 4:18

So we fix our eyes not on
what is seen,
but on what is unseen,
since what is seen is temporary,
but what is unseen is eternal.

TODAY IS _____

THANK YOU, LORD FOR:

PEOPLE IN NEED OF PRAYER

ANSWERED PRAYER:

WORKING ON:

SCRIPTURE:

CALLS TO ACTION
(WHO WILL I SERVE/UPLIFT TODAY?)

SONGS/HYMNS:

The name of
the Lord is
a fortified tower;
the righteous run to it
and are safe.

PROVERBS 18:10

TODAY IS _____

DEAR GOD,
THANK YOU FOR:

PEOPLE TO PRAY FOR:

SCRIPTURE READING:

SCRIPTURE REFLECTION:

SELF IMPROVEMENT:

LONG TERM GOALS:

SHORT TERM GOALS:

**SEEK THE LORD
WHILE HE MAY BE
FOUND;
CALL UPON HIM
WHILE HE IS NEAR.**

ISAIAH 55:6

TODAY IS _____

DEAR GOD,

AND WE KNOW THAT IN ALL THINGS GOD WORKS FOR THE GOOD OF THOSE WHO LOVE HIM, WHO HAVE BEEN CALLED ACCORDING TO HIS PURPOSE.

ROMANS 8:28

TODAY IS _____

THANK YOU, LORD FOR:

PEOPLE IN NEED OF PRAYER

ANSWERED PRAYER:

WORKING ON:

SCRIPTURE:

SONGS/HYMNS:

CALLS TO ACTION
(WHO WILL I SERVE/UPLIFT TODAY?)

ISAIAH 41:13

For I am the LORD your God who takes hold of your right hand and says to you, "Do not fear; I will help you."

TODAY IS _____

DEAR GOD,
THANK YOU FOR:

PEOPLE TO PRAY FOR:

SCRIPTURE READING:

SCRIPTURE REFLECTION:

SELF IMPROVEMENT:

LONG TERM GOALS:

SHORT TERM GOALS:

IF ANY OF YOU LACKS WISDOM, YOU SHOULD ASK GOD, WHO GIVES GENEROUSLY TO ALL WITHOUT FINDING FAULT, AND IT WILL BE GIVEN TO YOU.

JAMES 1:5

TODAY IS _____

DEAR GOD,

If my people, who are called by my name, will humble themselves and pray and seek my face and turn from their wicked ways, then I will hear from heaven, and I will forgive their sin and will heal their land.

2 CHRONICLES 7:14

TODAY IS _____

THANK YOU, LORD FOR:

PEOPLE IN NEED OF PRAYER

ANSWERED PRAYER:

WORKING ON:

SCRIPTURE:

CALLS TO ACTION
(WHO WILL I SERVE/UPLIFT TODAY?)

SONGS/HYMNS:

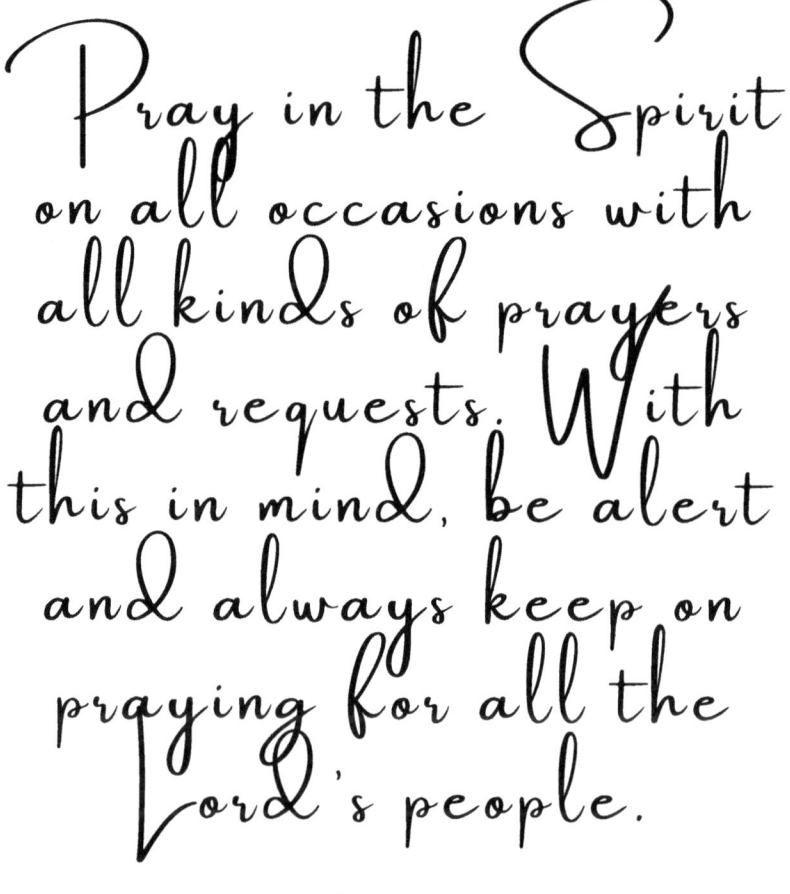

Pray in the Spirit on all occasions with all kinds of prayers and requests. With this in mind, be alert and always keep on praying for all the Lord's people.

EPHESIANS 6:18

TODAY IS _____

DEAR GOD,
THANK YOU FOR:

PEOPLE TO PRAY FOR:

SCRIPTURE READING:

SCRIPTURE REFLECTION:

SELF IMPROVEMENT:

LONG TERM GOALS:

SHORT TERM GOALS:

WHEN YOU PASS THROUGH
THE WATERS,
I WILL BE WITH YOU;
AND WHEN YOU PASS
THROUGH THE RIVERS, THEY
WILL NOT SWEEP OVER YOU.
WHEN YOU WALK THROUGH
THE FIRE, YOU WILL NOT BE
BURNED; THE FLAMES WILL
NOT SET YOU ABLAZE.

ISAIAH 43:2

TODAY IS _____

DEAR GOD,
_____
_____
_____
_____
_____
_____
_____
_____
_____
_____
_____
_____
_____
_____
_____
_____
_____
_____
_____
_____

BUT I TELL YOU, LOVE YOUR ENEMIES AND PRAY FOR THOSE WHO PERSECUTE YOU.

MATTHEW 5:44

TODAY IS _____

THANK YOU, LORD FOR:

PEOPLE IN NEED OF PRAYER

ANSWERED PRAYER:

WORKING ON:

SCRIPTURE:

CALLS TO ACTION
(WHO WILL I SERVE/UPLIFT TODAY?)

SONGS/HYMNS:

And our hope for you is firm, because we know that just as you share in our sufferings, so also you share in our comfort.

2 CORINTHIANS 1:7

TODAY IS _____

DEAR GOD,
THANK YOU FOR:

PEOPLE TO PRAY FOR:

SCRIPTURE READING:

SCRIPTURE REFLECTION:

SELF IMPROVEMENT:

LONG TERM GOALS:

SHORT TERM GOALS:

THIS IS THE
CONFIDENCE WE HAVE
IN APPROACHING GOD:
THAT IF WE ASK
ANYTHING ACCORDING
TO HIS WILL,
HE HEARS US.

1 JOHN 5:14

TODAY IS _____

DEAR GOD,

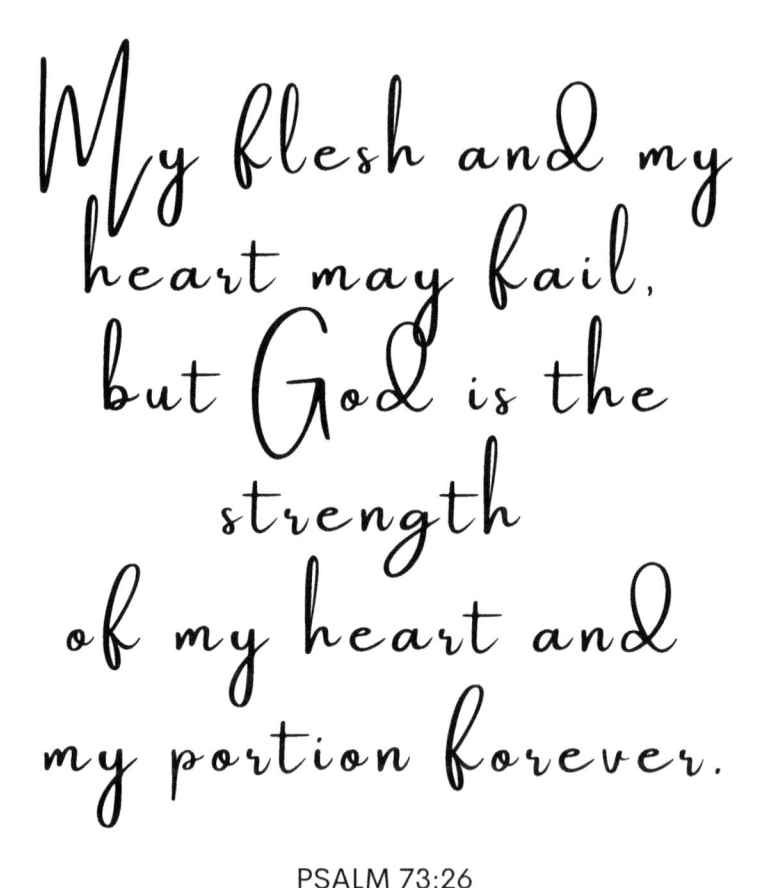

My flesh and my heart may fail, but God is the strength of my heart and my portion forever.

PSALM 73:26

TODAY IS _____

THANK YOU, LORD FOR:

PEOPLE IN NEED OF PRAYER

ANSWERED PRAYER:

WORKING ON:

SCRIPTURE:

CALLS TO ACTION
(WHO WILL I SERVE/UPLIFT TODAY?)

SONGS/HYMNS:

THE LORD IS MY STRENGTH AND MY SHIELD; MY HEART TRUSTED IN HIM, AND I AM HELPED: THEREFORE, MY HEART GREATLY REJOICETH; AND WITH MY SONG WILL I PRAISE HIM.

PSALMS 28:7

TODAY IS _____

DEAR GOD,
THANK YOU FOR:

PEOPLE TO PRAY FOR:

SCRIPTURE READING:

SCRIPTURE REFLECTION:

SELF IMPROVEMENT:

LONG TERM GOALS:

SHORT TERM GOALS:

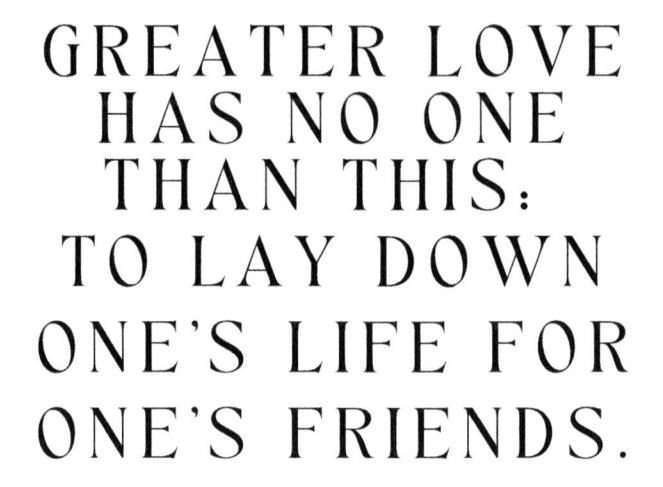

GREATER LOVE
HAS NO ONE
THAN THIS:
TO LAY DOWN
ONE'S LIFE FOR
ONE'S FRIENDS.

JOHN 15:13

TODAY IS _____

DEAR GOD, _____

_____

_____

_____

_____

_____

_____

_____

_____

_____

_____

_____

_____

_____

_____

_____

_____

_____

1 PETER 2:24

He himself bore our sins in his body on the cross, so that we might die to sins and live for righteousness; By his wounds you have been Healed.

TODAY IS _____

THANK YOU, LORD FOR:

PEOPLE IN NEED OF PRAYER

ANSWERED PRAYER:

WORKING ON:

SCRIPTURE:

CALLS TO ACTION
(WHO WILL I SERVE/UPLIFT TODAY?)

SONGS/HYMNS:

THE LORD MAKES FIRM THE STEPS OF THE ONE WHO DELIGHTS IN HIM; THOUGH HE MAY STUMBLE, HE WILL NOT FALL, FOR THE LORD UPHOLDS HIM WITH HIS HAND.

PSALM 37:23-24

TODAY IS _____

DEAR GOD,
THANK YOU FOR:

PEOPLE TO PRAY FOR:

SCRIPTURE READING:

SCRIPTURE REFLECTION:

SELF IMPROVEMENT:

LONG TERM GOALS:

SHORT TERM GOALS:

Is anyone among you
in trouble?
Let them pray.
Is anyone happy?
Let them sing songs
of praise.

JAMES 5:13

TODAY IS _____

DEAR GOD, _____

CERTIFICATE

OF COMMITMENT

FOR

PRAYER WARRIOR

Proudly presented to

_____

"THE EFFECTIVE PRAYER OF A RIGHTEOUS PERSON ACCOMPLISHES MUCH."

JAMES 5:16

Printed in Great Britain
by Amazon